MW01124918

P2T

Preparing 2 Thrive

in the Modern Workplace

By Jonathan L. Isaacson

Resources For Young Pros,
Book One

Copyright © 2024 by Jonathan L. Isaacson
All rights reserved

This book or any portion thereof may not be
reproduced, transmitted in any form or by any
means (electronic, mechanical, photocopying,
recording, or otherwise) or used in any manner
whatsoever without the prior, express written
permission of the author, except for the use of
brief quotations in a book review.

Printed in the United States of America
First Printing, 2024
IBSN 978-1-7356227-8-1

Published by The DYOJO
thedyojo.com

Library of Congress Control Number: 2024900242

Early Testimonials

P2T doesn't just challenge the status quo but offers real-world equations and examples of ways to grow and improve throughout your professional journey. - Michelle Blevins, Cleaning & Restoration Magazine

I like the Three Be's. I like the candor. *P2T* feels like the author is writing a letter to their younger self. - David Princeton, Advocate Claim Service

The Three Be's of success are perfect reminders for all of us that with a little hard work, honesty, and willingness to learn, we can equip ourselves with a framework to achieve success. - Benjamin Ricciardi, Ironclad Restoration Marketing

This is a book that every young person should read. *P2T* will also help tons of others who need a reminder of what it takes to succeed, and the mindset needed to achieve their goals. - Rico Garcia, Jr., Restoration Domination

If you want the young people around you to dream big and have the tools to achieve their goals, then tune into *P2T*. - Josh Diaz, Robotics Account Manager

Jon Isaacson's engaging and practical writing style, coupled with his focus on self-reflection, goal-setting, and taking on new challenges, makes *P2T* a valuable for personal and professional growth. - Thea Tapson, Estimator

Great practical advice for young people entering the workforce. I enjoyed *P2T*. - Tatsuya "Tats" Nakagawa, Castagra

I love that Jon wrote **P2T**. As a service business owner, one of the things that kept me up at night was wondering if I would be able to attract young people to join my organization to work and start a career. Jon is doing the important work. - Eric Sprague, Super Tech University

If you are a young professional struggling with your purpose, or where you're trying to go in life, I recommend you start with **P2T!** - Dave Luce, LAQ Environmental

P2T will help young people enter the workforce because it gives them the opportunity to see that anyone can do great things. Our students need to know that they can do any and everything regardless of their situation as long as they have **The Three Be's**. - Bre Brown, College & Career Specialist

Jon is a restoration industry icon, not only as a restoration contractor but as one who uses his experience and knowledge to better the industry with podcasts and literature. Everyone will pick up something from **P2T**. - Mitch Heitman, Regional Vice President

If you are a young professional, **P2T** is a must-have book. The author has come up from the property restoration ranks; from the entry-level position of sucking water to co-owner of his own restoration company. His insight into the skilled trades and career growth make this book a must-read! - Keith Nelson, Commercial Project Consultant Manager

Young professionals want to focus on building their life and using work as a tool for the resources needed. It is about working to live and not living to work, this theme resonates in **P2T**. - Kristy Cohen, CEO

Jon has a gift for capturing thoughts and skills and putting them into words. If young professionals act on the words of wisdom in *P2T* they can skyrocket their career to the next level. - David Watts, Regional Manager

As the author outlines in *P2T*, small steps taken day-by-day combined with having a positive attitude will help young people be happy and healthy. - Marin Caba, Business Owner, American Water Damage Restoration

The information in this book is very useful and even made me reflect on the way I run my business. It is very clear to read and straight to the point. I can't wait to make my kids read *P2T*. - Elan Pasmanick, Born to Repair

Jon tells it like it is. I even felt motivated to work even harder and want my teenage son to read *P2T* to understand why effort and education matter, especially for those who are still in high school. - Amy Markwood, eLearning Consultant

P2T is applicable to those in school, entering the workforce, and honestly those in the workforce now. - Toni Neary, Director of Community Engagement and Workforce Innovation

The style utilized in *P2T* hits a happy nerve in my mind and allows me to easily read the information. This book inspires me to learn. - Rob MacPherson, Manager of Training and Development

P2T helps the reader identify key personality traits for success. - Bill Wilson, author

Table of Contents

Intro

Two types of people will receive and read this book, we call them Young Professional A (YPA) and Young Professional B (YPB). At the start of their career, there isn't much that separates YPA from YPB. They both have few **resources**, little work **experience**, and low **knowledge** about the working world.

Both young professionals are going to struggle to get a job.

Both young professionals have people that care about them. The difference is that one of these young professionals will listen to what the good influences around them were saying.

The young professional with the right roadmap and the willingness to learn will set themselves up for success.

**_P2T_ creates win-wins
for employers and employees.**

P2T is Book 1 in the *Resources for Young Pros* series. Organizations win when their young professionals are engaged. Young pros win when they have a roadmap for success.

The stories, examples, and principles shared in this book are from real world experience. *P2T* will prepare readers to *thrive* in the modern workplace.

Prepared to *thrive* in any job interview.

Prepared to *thrive* in any new job.

Prepared to *thrive* as emerging professionals.

**Employers will be handing *P2T* out
by the DOZENS to new hires.**

Book Structure

The chapters contain the main content. In between each chapter are various sub-chapters to challenge and encourage readers in their journey.

Nearsighted deals with preparing for the interview process.

Farsighted deals with items that help new employees set themselves up for success at work.

The reader can complete the text cover to cover or refer to specific chapters as needed.

Young professionals who want to earn more,
first need to learn more.

Book Purpose

Audience. This book was written to help young professionals develop the mindsets and habits to thrive in the modern workplace. Anyone who is applying for their first job, starting their career, or trying to advance at work will receive value from reading this book.

To those preparing to thrive in the workplace, we are rooting for you.

Value. Anyone encouraging young professionals, from family members to business owners, will find this book is an excellent resource. The principles from each chapter are applicable to success in work and life. Business owners will be handing out this book by the dozens to young professionals they interview and hire.

To those helping young professionals thrive, we salute you.

Thrive (verb)

*To progress toward
or realize a goal
despite or because
of circumstances.*

1 Thrive or Survive?

If you are applying for jobs, Chapters 4 - 10 will help you develop tools to stand out and survive the interview process.

If you are a new employee, this book will help you develop the mindsets and habits to *thrive* in the modern workplace.

Most of the young professionals receiving this book will be those who are being interviewed or hired by companies that are investing in their people. If a company representative, hiring manager, or supervisor gave you this book, it's a good sign. It means you are working for a company that wants you to be successful.

> This is unique.

> It means there is a good chance you will be more than just a number.

Getting a job and growing your career falls under what most people call **professional development**. This means building skills that apply to being a better worker. Thriving at work is a win-win. The company wins because you become more engaged and valuable to them. You win by earning more responsibility and gaining better opportunities at work.

Yes, more responsibility and better opportunities mean more money.

If you want more than a paycheck, this book is for you.

If you want to *thrive* at work and in life, this book is for you.

What does it mean to thrive?

Thrive (verb)

To grow vigorously; flourish.

To gain in wealth or possessions; prosper.

To progress toward or realize a goal despite or because of circumstances.

Your professional skills increase as you increase your **knowledge**, grow your **experiences**, and develop your **abilities**. Three of the four key elements we will discuss throughout this book.

As you grow your skills you elevate your confidence.

As your confidence legitimately grows, so does your value and access to new opportunities and **resources**.

This book will help you understand the mindsets and habits you will need to *thrive* in the modern workplace.

My mission in life is not

merely to survive,

but to thrive;

and to do so

with some passion,

some compassion,

some humor,

and some style.

Maya Angelou

Internal and External

As you prepare to *thrive* in the modern workplace, we are going to discuss *internal* growth and *external* opportunities.

Internal development is what happens inside of you. You have direct control over the effort you invest to grow your knowledge, experience, and abilities. Your actions affect your outcomes.

External development is what happens outside of you. You do not control your outcomes, but good things happen when people notice you are growing as a person. Professional development expands your access to resources to help you continue to grow.

2 A Solid Foundation

Every great structure starts with a solid foundation. If you want to build a life that is deeply rooted and a career that will weather the storms of life, you need a solid foundation. Your foundation for thriving in the modern workplace starts with three-character traits.

The Three Be's
> Be honest
>> Be hardworking
>>> Be willing to learn

Every employer values these three traits.

Every person who has made something of their life would agree that these three traits played a role in their development.

What does it mean to be honest?

Internally, it means being honest with yourself. It means recognizing where you are so that you can move toward where you want to be (see Chapter 11, *The Three Where's*).

Externally, it means doing what you said you would do. If you mess up, you own it. If you make a mistake and an employer asks about it, you acknowledge the error (see Chapter 20, *Making Mistakes*).

Most employers respect honesty. Most employers will respect you even more if you can tell them what you did wrong and how you plan to prevent it from happening again.

No one expects you to be perfect. But you will help yourself in the long run if you can be relied upon to be someone with integrity.

Be honest with yourself and with others.

What does it mean to be hardworking?

Internally, it means working your butt off to reach your goals. You are accountable to yourself. Are you doing the things you need to do to increase your **knowledge**, **experience**, and **abilities** (see Chapters 13 - 17)?

Externally, it means showing up. You can't work hard if you are always late or never arrive. It means being teachable and doing your best to improve. If people don't believe you are trying, they will not go out of their way to help you.

No one expects you to know it all. But you will help yourself in the long run if you can be relied upon to be someone who shows up and gives their 100% effort.

Be hardworking and doors will open.

What does it mean to be willing to learn?

Internally, it means listening and observing. It means applying new knowledge to your life experiences.

Externally, it means building trust. When people see that you listen and do your best to learn, they are invested in teaching you more.

No one expects you to be perfect. But you will help yourself in the long run if you can be relied upon to be someone who is teachable.

Be willing to learn and people will be willing to teach you.

The Three Be's at Work

As an employer, I have hired, trained, and promoted numerous young people who came to my businesses with little to no prior skills.

There is no prior skill required to be honest, hardworking, or willing to learn.

There is no limit to what you can accomplish if you are honest, hardworking, and willing to learn.

If a person is honest, hardworking, and willing to learn, an employer can teach *anyone* to be successful in *anything*. On the other hand, if a person is <u>not</u> willing to be honest, hardworking, or willing to learn, there is little that anyone can do for them.

Perspective plays a big part in your ability to ***thrive***.

The Three Be's

The Three Be's

<u>Be</u> honest

<u>Be</u> hardworking

<u>Be</u> willing to learn

Two Young Pros - 3B's

Let's contrast and compare two young professionals applying the principles in this book. What would they look like if they were practicing opposite sides of **The Three Be's**?

Young Professional A

Being honest
Understands where they are starting from
Does their best to tell the truth to others

Hardworking
Shows up and does what they say, gives advance notice if something changes
Each day they try to be better than the last

Willing to Learn
Listens and follows through
They want to earn more so they are committed to learn more

Young Professional B

Entitled
They think the world owes them something
Says what they think needs to be said in the moment

Unreliable
Often late or doesn't show up
When they do show up they aren't focused, they find ways to have other people do their work

Un-coachable
Has to be told the same information multiple times
Expects more money without taking on more responsibility

3 How You See Things

Your perspective is also called your worldview. How you see the world, your role in it, and your opportunities affect what you think is possible.

When someone struggles with vision, they usually have one of two issues. They can be *nearsighted*. This means they can't see very well unless the item is close to their eyes. Or they can be *farsighted*. Meaning they see better when objects are further away.

When we apply this to the desire to achieve basic goals, many people have the same vision issues.

How many people do you know that want something **right now** but can't see how they are acting is affecting their ability to obtain it?

What are some examples of this disconnect?

If a friend told you that they want to drive a car. They want the freedom of the open road. But they don't know how to achieve this goal. What would you tell them?

The conversation would probably start with figuring out how to get a driver's license, right?

In most states, one needs to be 18 years old and take two tests. First, a written exam and complete a driving test. For those under the age of 18 years old, there is usually a driver's education process that prepares the student for these two requirements.

What if your friend refused to take the driver's course?

What if they signed up for the course but never showed up for class?

What if they showed up for class but they didn't pay attention or they were obnoxious during the training?

Would your friend's actions affect their ability to achieve their goal? They said one thing, but their actions didn't help them move any closer to success.

Can we agree that our actions affect our outcomes?

If we agree on this point, then we can agree that achieving goals requires us to have the right perspective. Not just seeing what's in front of you. Not only looking for what's further down your path. But learning and taking action.

Do you have the right-sightedness to prepare to *thrive* in the modern workplace?

Uncomfortable

Getting my license was a benchmark moment. It meant I had new freedoms, but it also meant I had new responsibilities. The deal was I had to pay for my gas and my car insurance. If I wanted the freedom of driving, I would need to earn enough to cover my expenses.

If memory serves:

My insurance was $88.00 per month
Gas was $0.97 a gallon
The minimum wage was $5.15 per hour

I needed at least 20 hours a month to pay insurance, which didn't include gas or any kind of fun money.

Across from my junior high, and not that far from my house, was a burger joint called *Woody's*. I knocked on the window and asked to speak to the owner. I was nervous, but I took a risk and asked her what I would need to do to get a job. I didn't have a grand plan, but I showed up, I asked questions, and I listened.

Trying new things is uncomfortable. Without discomfort, there is no growth. Little did I know, as I awkwardly worked my way through the discomfort of this interview, I was meeting someone who would have a profound impact on my life: *Sharon*.

Sharon

Sharon (sitting in the middle) and her family
outside of Woody's (Moses Lake, WA).
Her daughter Jody, who now runs Woody's,
shared this photo with me when
I told her about the book.

<u>Nea</u>rsighted

This section deals with immediate challenges related to applying, interviewing, and acquiring a job.

4 Interviews

If you have an interview coming up, congratulations. If this is one of your first interviews, you may be stressing out. Remember, your actions affect your outcomes, so you should be as prepared as possible. Taking the right action does not guarantee the outcomes you desire but it will set you up for success.

It's good to dress the part, be ready for any question an employer could ask you and have a nice resume with quality references ready. Even with all this, you may not get the job.

Unfortunately, this is part of life.

Each time you try, as well as each time you fail, it is a **learning experience**. If you are willing to learn, each difficult lesson teaches you something about being more prepared for the next opportunity.

Failure is a part of building your work and life experience.

For those who are preparing for an interview soon, here are some quick tips to help you stand out from your peers.

Tips for Thriving in a Job Interview

Read and re-read the job description
Research the company
Prepare a cover letter and references
Prepare your own questions
Rehearse the interview
Dress the part
Don't be afraid to ask questions

Dress the Part

In years past, people wore suits and dresses to interviews to try to impress the company. In my era, business casual was more the norm. Nowadays, it is the organization's preference.

You can ask a company representative what you should wear to the interview. Or you could go by during business hours and see what most of the employees wear. It can be helpful to look like you fit in with the current team culture, but it can also be an advantage to dress up a bit to make an impression.

Generally, business casual is a safe bet. This means dressing nicer than your daily wear. Slacks and a collared (polo) shirt with clean shoes and combed hair. Look like you want the job, not like you just were hanging out with your friends.

5 The Job Description

When a company writes a job description, they are giving applicants clues about what they are looking for. You shouldn't have to dig too deep into the job description to find a few things that you understand and relate to the knowledge, experience, and abilities you have demonstrated in your life (see Chapter 12 for more on these *Four Elements*).

What is the title of the position? If the title is something like *entry-level customer service representative*, what does this tell you?

Entry-level usually means that they are hiring someone with little to no prior experience.

Customer service can mean many things, but it usually requires the employees to interact directly with the public.

Read what the listing says about a few key elements.

Qualifications. This is where they tell you what prior knowledge, experience, and/or abilities they expect applicants to have.

Roles and/or responsibilities. This is where they try to paint a picture of what applicants will be doing if they get hired.

Compensation. Some organizations will tell you what the salary or hourly wage range is, and others will not.

You will want to try to determine if the **qualifications** are required or recommended. For example, the employer may *prefer* that you have an associate degree (AA/AS) but they don't *require* it. Even if they say they require a degree, you may roll the dice and apply anyway.

What experiences do you have that are relevant to the **roles and responsibilities** outlined in the job description? If you have demonstrated knowledge, experience, or abilities that could be worth more than a degree, you will want to use the <u>cover letter</u> to communicate this.

If they don't specify the **compensation**, this is a question you can ask in the interview. Asking, "How much does this job pay," is a reasonable question. Instead, try asking it another way. For example, "Is the compensation rate at or above minimum wage?" Sounds a little more intelligent. Then you can follow up with, "What is the process and timeline for becoming eligible for a promotion."

This approach communicates that you understand that if you **work hard**, you will earn more. Some jobs have a review after 90 days. Others may provide training or certification that opens up more pathways to greater responsibilities and higher pay.

Be proud of the fact that you want to ***thrive***. You should leave the interview with a sense of clarity about what your options for advancement are.

6 Research the Company

Research is easy. Does the company have a website, social media, or articles written about them? Review whatever is available, so you have an idea of what you are walking into at your interview. Pay attention to what they say about their mission, vision, and/or values (MVV).

My construction company is called ARES. If you were applying to this company, where would you start to look for information about what we do and what we think makes us unique?

You might ask, what does ARES stand for?

> **A**dvanced
> **R**estoration
> **E**nvironmental
> **S**ervices

What are restoration and environmental services?

The first page of the company website states, "ARES are the experts in helping you navigate the insurance claim repairs process in the event of damage to your home or business from fire or flooding. Based in Graham, Washington, our team has been working with homeowners throughout Pierce, Kitsap, and Thurston Counties to empower you in the process of *Giving You Back Your Home*[i]."

With this minimal look at a company website, what do we know that might help us crush it during an interview?

> Their name starts with Advanced, and they think of themselves as experts

> They provide insurance claim repairs

They fix homes and businesses following fire and water damages

They are based in Graham and serve three counties

Their tagline is *Giving You Back Your Home*

Many companies start their interview with some variation of, *"Why do you want to work here?"* If you can convey that you have done some research and have an idea that you want to be a part of something specific that they are doing, you can set yourself apart. Don't overthink it, use their own words.

So, if I asked you, *"Why do you want to work at ARES?"*

What would you say?

Some answers that would help you stand out would include: Compliment the organization with their own catchphrases.

"I noticed your name starts with Advanced and you state that you are experts. I would like to be a part of an organization that excels at what they do. At my last job, I worked hard to be the best that I could be in my role. One time I received an award or praise from my supervisor for _____ (insert activity) and that felt good to do something at a high level of quality and be recognized for my effort." You are showing that you know something about the company and tying your experience to pursuing a shared outcome.

Highlight one of their values that aligns with your own interests.

"I noticed you are based in Graham and active in your community. It is important to me to be a part of a company that gives back to the community. In high school, I was able to _____(insert community activity) and this made a big impression on me." It may sound like a humble brag, but this is a competition. You are competing with other applicants to win this job. You want to set yourself apart, especially if you can do so by linking your prior experiences to the values of the company.

Express a genuine interest in what the company does.

If anyone you know had an experience with water or fire damage in their home, you might discuss what you noticed about that experience. Or you might ask, *"Your tagline is 'giving you back your home,' what does that look like in what you do?"* Asking informed questions can be an excellent way to get the interviewer talking about their company and themselves. Listen and take mental notes to help you ask additional questions.

If you want to **thrive**, come prepared for the interview.

7 Cover Letters & References

A <u>cover letter</u> is a good way to communicate that you are serious about the job. A generic cover letter is okay, but it is much better to write a unique cover letter for each job that you are applying for.

Take a few highlights from the job description and a few points from the company research to personalize your cover letter. This is similar to the examples in the prior chapter.

First paragraph

Two or three sentences that provide a quick introduction to who you are and a few highlights from your professional achievements. Only use as many words as you need to make your points. In my opinion, a one-page cover letter is best unless you truly need more room to make your case.

Second paragraph

Three or four sentences that demonstrate you understand the company's vision and values. Tie in wording that shows you have some relevant experiences related to the job responsibilities.

Third paragraph

Two or three sentences that tie everything together. "I look forward to the opportunity to work with a team that is so respected in our community for _____ (insert an attribute of the company). I believe my prior experiences and abilities will enable me to be a quick learner and asset to your efforts to _____ (insert a goal or need from the job description)."

There's a good chance whoever reviews your resume only looks at the first and last paragraph, so those are important areas of focus for you.

References

It is good to have a list of 3-5 professional <u>references</u> who can speak to your character as a person and your value as an employee.

When you apply for a job, having a list of three personal references can help you stand out from your peers. The best references are people who observed you in a supervisory capacity. People who will speak positively about your character and work-related experiences. Friends and family are not typically the best references as they are viewed as biased. A teacher, coach, volunteer coordinator, or prior employer are examples of quality references.

It's always a good idea to ask these people if they would be willing to be a reference. It's also a good idea to give them a heads-up if you have listed them as a reference so that they can be mentally prepared when they receive a call from an employer.

Letters of Recommendation

You can boost the impact of your professional references by asking these individuals for letters of recommendation. This is a reference that they write down so that you can share it with employers.

8 Ask Questions

Asking questions is one of the best ways you can demonstrate you have come prepared. What questions should you ask? I think it is helpful to understand that every company solves a problem. If you understand the problem they want to solve, you can discuss topics that should be important to the company representatives you are interviewing with.

Let's review some employment scenarios to determine what challenges they embrace.

My uncle was a homebuilder. What problem did his company solve? That's easy, it built homes for people who needed (or wanted) them.

What problem does a fast-food drive-through, like the one I worked at in high school, solve? It provides ready-to-consume food-like products to people on the go.

I went to work in a rehabilitation facility as a nurse's aide. What problem did this organization solve? It provided medical services to people who couldn't care for themselves as well as rehabilitation for people recovering from medical procedures.

How would you determine what problem the organization is trying to solve?

If you want to know what problem the organization you are applying to is working to solve, you can access their website or social media profile to see what they advertise. The company bio, introductory videos, and latest posts will provide you with information that you can use to sound intelligent during your interview.

>What is the company tagline?

>Does the company have a frequently asked questions (FAQs) page?

>What was the last video that they posted?

>What did they say in their last social media post?

When you get close to the end of your interview, the interviewer will ask if you have any questions for them. If you don't ask any questions, you will have missed <u>two opportunities</u>.

>The first opportunity is to gain the answers to the questions about the company or position.

>The second opportunity is to impress the interviewer with the research you did.

Asking questions shows effort. It shows that you like to be informed and care about understanding the company's mission and values.

Listening, researching, and asking intelligent questions are all important tools if you want to *thrive* in the modern workplace.

Learning from Failure

If you have applied to multiple jobs and been to several interviews but aren't getting a call back, it's time to take an honest look at your approach. Ask yourself, "What could I do more effectively?"

It may feel like you're being treated unfairly. But focusing on what others are doing isn't going to get you anywhere. **You can only control what you can control.** You can adapt your approach.

Option 1. Call a company that rejected you and politely ask for feedback. "I'm trying to learn how to interview better, could you please tell me how I could have improved my approach?" You may not get feedback but it's worth the effort.

Option 2. Try new things and see how they work out. It could be something as simple as combing your hair, wearing a different shirt, or updating your cover letter. Usually, it comes down to convincing people you are worth the risk. You do this by building your confidence, listening, and demonstrating that you can be an asset to their team.

Option 3. Ask someone you trust, someone who will give your honest feedback, to play back the process and give their viewpoint.

There is a lot of competition for many of these open positions, you must find ways to make yourself stand out.

9 Direct vs Relevant Experience

If you have not had a job before, you will not have **direct** experience. Direct experience means experience with the roles, responsibilities, and skills of the job. Even if you have some work experience, you likely won't have a lot of direct experience in for the position you are applying for.

This does not mean that you are without **relevant** experience.

You need to understand the business so that you can identify and communicate your relevant experiences. Refer back to the prior chapters for ways you can learn more about the company you are applying for.

For example, if a restaurant was hiring someone to take orders, prepare food, and clean the restaurant, they likely want people with direct experience with each of these tasks. If you have this experience, you will want to highlight this in your resume and during the interview.

If you do not have direct experience, you will need to think about what relevant **knowledge**, **experience**, and **abilities** you have. Relevant, or indirect, experience means that you have done work like the type of work that you would be doing for the organization.

Taking orders. Maybe you have no direct experience with taking orders in a restaurant, but you did volunteer at your high school concession stand where you took a high volume of orders from students, parents, and community members. *Relevant.*

Preparing food. Maybe you have no direct experience preparing food in a restaurant setting, but in your home economics class, your teacher commented on how well you followed the recipes and how clean you kept your workspace. *Relevant.*

Cleaning. Maybe you have no direct experience cleaning a business, but you have helped your coach clean the practice room following practice and raised money for your team by cleaning a local stadium after sporting events. *Relevant.*

When you start your work journey you will lack direct experience. Don't let this lack of direct experience discourage you from trying new things. Help yourself by thinking through what aspects of your relevant experience you can communicate to a potential employer.

Once you get a job, the process for advancement is similar in that you prove you can learn more. When you learn more, you earn more.

10 Rehearse

It's one thing for an actor to be prepared. It's another thing for them to deliver when it's showtime. When the curtain draws back and the bright lights turn on, a lot of people get stage fright.

If you get nervous or forget what you planned when you start an interview, you are not alone. One helpful way to offset this is to rehearse the interview with someone who has been involved in one before.

Even better, if you know someone who works at the organization or in a similar company, they can help you understand the process.

> How will you introduce yourself?

> Will you bring a resume, cover letter, and/or references?

> What questions do you think they will ask you?

> What questions do you want to ask?

A few sample questions might include an interviewer asking you to tell them about a time when you:

> *Disagreed with an adult or peer; how did you handle it?*

> *Overcame a challenging situation or circumstance.*

> *Witnessed someone do something wrong.*

> *Had to work with others on a team to meet a deadline.*

It's important to listen to the question. If you don't understand you can ask them politely to repeat it. These types of questions are intended to demonstrate you can think on your feet. It's good practice to keep your answers related to work scenarios.

For example, the first question above asks about a disagreement. You wouldn't want to bring up your last argument with your parents, no one needs to know about those personal issues. But, if you have no direct work experience, you could talk about a time when a coach got on you.

You might say, "At first, I didn't like what they had to say, but I realized they were right and when I did what they were telling me to do it helped me improve. Later in the season they even asked me to help other athletes who needed some extra help."

Most interviewers want to understand that you are a person of character.

>*Will you show up on time?*
>*Will you be responsible?*

They also want to know that you are capable of learning and performing the job.

>*Are you willing to learn?*
>*Have you had issues with authority?*

Most jobs will require that you work in a team setting.

Have you been a good team member in other settings?
>*Are you coachable?*

If you want to **thrive** in an interview, show them that you are honest, hardworking, and willing to learn.

Respect the Process

I shared my interview experience in the subchapter *Uncomfortable*. I got the job. I was making money, but I was also learning valuable lessons.

I learned a lot about how one person, working from a tiny burger shack, can help young people think differently about life.

I learned that doing things excellently didn't always mean a big paycheck.

I learned that everything had a process, to take pride in my work, to set money aside for the future, and to be a good human being.

I learned many habits that helped me at school, at work, and in life from my boss at the burger shop. In business, I have learned the value of standard operating procedures or SOPs.

I saw how work could be practiced as an art. A business operates so much more smoothly when there is a simple science driving the roles and responsibilities.

We had a set recipe so that our fry sauce tasted the same every time

We had specific knives with guides for cutting lettuce, onions, and tomatoes so they were consistent

We weighed and pre-packaged fried foods so the customer got a good value and we were profitable

*We had a system for cleaning and closing each night
so no item was left undone*

Sharon also taught me that setting aside a small portion of my check for longer-term savings could add up quickly without affecting my needs or taking away from my fun money.

Some people look down on retail or restaurant work. Sharon showed me that it could be meaningful work for all involved. She invested in people and her community. She made sacrifices to do so. I believe she did it because she found a greater purpose in helping others get their start.

'Hard-working' is what
gets the job done.
You just see that
year after year.
The students who thrive
are not necessarily
the ones who come in
with the perfect scores.
It's the ones who love
what they're doing
and go at it vigorously.

Carol S. Dweck

F<u>ar</u>sighted

*This section deals with preparing to thrive
in the modern workplace.
We will discuss principles that help you build
a foundation and set yourself up to advance
in any workplace.*

Resighted

11 Who, What, Where

We've discussed some tips for thriving in an interview. These principles should help you compete better during the hiring process. Now we will turn our attention to ways to **thrive** once you have a job.

WHO you are is a key factor in getting WHAT you want.

Are you familiar with the often-quoted question from William Shakespeare's tragic play Romeo and Juliet?

"O Romeo, Romeo! Wherefore art thou Romeo?"

While we often hear, *"Where art thou Romeo."* The question his lover asks is *"Wherefore art thou?"* She is not simply asking *where* are you? She is asking something deeper. She is asking *why* are you.

In their story, there is a lot of drama between families. These complications build until the tragic end of many characters in the story (I won't ruin it all if you aren't familiar with the whole story). What is the difference between *where* you are, *who* you are, and *why* you are?

<u>Where</u> you came from impacts your vision of where you are headed.

<u>Who</u> you were raised around impacts your perception of what goals you can achieve.

If you are going to thrive you must confront <u>why</u> you believe what you believe.

You are invested in finding ways to thrive in the modern workplace. How do I know that without knowing you? I know it because not a lot of people take the time to read. But here you are. You would not be reading this book if you weren't serious.

If you want to get beyond what you think is possible, you will have to answer Juliet's question, "Wherefore art thou." Meaning you will have to start with where you are, but you will also need to discover who you are as well as why you are.

The Three Where's

Where #1 = Where I am

Where #2 = Where I will be

Where #3 = Where I want to be

"Wherefore art thou?"

If you aren't where you want to be in life, you will need to recognize who you are now (where #1). Growing from who you are now, to who you want to be, will move you closer to where you want to be.

Thriving starts with taking action from <u>where</u>ver you are. The longer you hesitate to act, the longer you will remain in the first two *where's*. To successfully transition from where you are to where you want to be, you need to be honest about your current level of **knowledge**, **experience**, **abilities**, and **resources** so that you can learn to develop them further.

Let's discuss these **Four Elements** of personal and professional development.

Mindset and Habits

Committing yourself to personal development means daily following through with your mindsets and habits.

You have to feed, seed, and pull the weeds
(see Chapter 14) if you are going
to blossom into the person you want to be.

Thriving is not just a destination,
it's a process (see Chapter 22).

12 Superpowers

It can feel like you need superpowers to get your first opportunity. So many young people that I talk to express frustration that a job listing says "entry-level" but the qualifications are too much.

If you want to *thrive* in the modern workplace, you first need the foundation. Do you remember what the foundation is built with? **The Three Be's** (see Chapter 2). Once the foundation is laid, you need to build the structure or the skeleton. There are **Four Elements** you will need to set yourself up for success.

> **Knowledge**
> **Experience**
> **Abilities**
> **Resources**

In the 1990's a unique kind of superhero emerged. He was summoned by five young people from five continents with five powerful rings. Whenever Earth was in trouble, they used their rings to call upon the hero with the green mullet. Earth, fire, water, wind, and heart would combine to create *Captain Planet*.

The underlying message was that when people from various backgrounds come together, they can solve earth's greatest needs.

When you combine knowledge, experience, abilities, and resources, you can advance your life and career.

Do you have a special ring like the Planeteers? Probably not, but you have this book. If you want to thrive, you will need to see the world through a growth mindset. Life's challenges also bring opportunities.

Everyone starting out has a professional stat sheet that looks like this:

Knowledge: **Low**
Experience: **Low**
Abilities: **Low**
Resources: **Low**

If you are honest, you recognize that you are **low** in all four elements. The good news is that 1) there is only one way to go, upward; and 2) everyone starts in the same place you are starting.

When Captain Planet was summoned, he would fly in with a booming voice, *"By your powers combined, I am Captain Planet! The power is yours!"* If you are willing to learn and apply the principles in this book you will unlock the power to face your challenges.

The power to increase these **Four Elements** for thriving in the modern workplace is yours.

Starting Out Strong

Your level of **knowledge**, **experience**, and **abilities** are what employers are trying to assess when they interview. This is a frustrating reality because you need the job to gain those resources.

When you are trying to get a job, and you don't have a deep history of the **Four Elements**, focus on how you are committed to earning those. Focus on how you have demonstrated the **Three Be's** in other opportunities.

When you are starting a new job, it may be difficult to understand how you develop in your new role. Keep your eyes and ears open for opportunities to increase your knowledge, experience, and abilities. Take advantage of the **resources** to elevate the Four Elements.

13 Knowledge

Why would you want to increase your knowledge? Because increasing your knowledge increases your field of vision. Knowledge helps you better understand the here-and-now as. Knowledge helps you see the bigger picture.

**Increase your knowledge =
Increase your perspective of what is possible.**

If you make an internal commitment to increase your knowledge, you will believe more is possible. If you expand what you believe is possible you will elevate your desire to learn even more.

As you increase your knowledge, you will notice something happens externally as well. When you demonstrate you are willing to learn and that you have increased your knowledge people will be more willing to take chances on you.

Knowledge is power.

Knowledge is fuel.

Knowledge will shorten your DANG learning curve.

The only way to build confidence is to learn and apply new information. Good things happen when people see you hard at work learning and applying new information. As you demonstrate your willingness to learn, you will receive opportunities to increase your experiences.

You develop confidence (internal) and people develop trust (external).

In the journey of life, we are all learning together. As it relates to learning from others and from what is going on around us,

I have a favorite Proverb. It says, *"I applied my heart to what I observed and learned a lesson from what I saw[ii]."*

What does this mean? To me, "I applied my heart" means paying attention to what is going on around you. To be in a constant state of listening and looking for knowledge.

This sounds a lot like being willing to learn.

Observation is free. Deciding what mindsets and habits to emulate and which ones to ignore is a key element of shortening your DANG learning curve.

If you want to **earn** more, you will need to **learn** more.

"Knowing is not enough,

we must apply.

Willing is not enough,

we must do."

Bruce Lee

14 Carpe Diem

Have you heard the often-used Latin phrase, **carpe diem**? This phrase means *seize the day*.

From what I have been told, because I don't speak Latin, it more literally translates, "*Harvest the day*." To seize the day means to see an opportunity and put yourself in a position to pursue it.

Harvest the day is a cool way to phrase it because it means opportunities don't just come by chance. You can only harvest what has been planted and cared for. Therefore, if you want to harvest the day you have to be **hard at work** to ensure you have planted, watered, weeded, and cared for the crops.

Carpe Diem.
Harvest the day!

Farmers, agricultural professionals, ranchers, etc. are considered skilled tradespersons. I've been in the skilled trades all of my professional life within the construction sector. I enjoy the skilled trades because each day brings new challenges. What I think is cool about the broad term "skilled trades" is that it has at least a two-fold meaning:

Those who are in the skilled trades are developing *skills* (abilities) they apply toward making a life for themselves.

Anyone can learn the *skills* that are needed to be a successful member of the trades community.

Everyone has some natural talents, but to excel consistently requires hard work. People who are good at something, whether it's sports, art, music, business, working with people, or something else have all had to put the effort in to develop their skills. Much like reaping a harvest, moving toward your goals is often a series of small steps that add over time.

Prepare the ground.

Plant the seeds.

Water, feed, and weed the soil.

Early in my career I learned how a small habit can open big doors. When I first started in property restoration, my manager informed me that insurance companies pay our company based on what we document. This meant that the pictures I took in the field and the paperwork that I filled out were critical to our company being able to charge for our services.

When he told me this, I took it as a personal challenge to make sure that my paperwork was always dialed in.

At first, I would even rewrite everything I did after I got home from work. It didn't take me long to be offered raises and a promotion. I literally was able to make more money by simply making sure my handwriting was legible.

By doing something most of my co-workers hated, paperwork, and filling out every form my boss needed, I was able to build trust. A little bit of effort led to some big opportunities.

I took the approach that if I put extra work in, I would gain new knowledge and experience. Taking this risk helped me reduce the time it took me to *bridge the gap*.

Harvesting the day (*carpe diem*) looks like showing up every day with a willingness to learn. The simple act of showing up and persisting with the learning process exposes you to the opportunity to build your skills.

A lot of people miss out because they don't show up.

A lot of people have no *harvest* because they don't plant seeds.

Increasing Your Knowledge

Knowledge: **Increasing**
Experience: Low
Abilities: Low
Resources: Low

How are you planting and caring for the seeds that will increase your knowledge?

<u>If you are preparing for an interview</u>
The thing that will stand out the most is highlighting your knowledge of what the company's value is to the marketplace. What do you know about the company and how do you see yourself adding value to their team? Review Chapters 4-10 for more ideas on how you can prepare for an interview.

<u>If you are trying to advance at work</u>
Acquiring new knowledge means looking for opportunities to learn. The company may have manuals or videos that help you learn more about their products and services. Listening to your supervisors, paying attention in meetings, and applying the things that other employees are teaching you are all excellent ways to increase your knowledge.

15 Wisdom

There is what you need to know (knowledge) and how to best apply that information to your life (wisdom). Wisdom often comes with experience. I heard a funny analogy on the difference between knowledge and wisdom.

Knowledge is knowing that a tomato is a fruit,
not a vegetable.

Wisdom is knowing that it doesn't
belong in a fruit salad.

I will borrow another analogy from a famous storyteller[iii] to demonstrate this reality. If knowledge were a seed, imagine a farmer in ancient times (before modern technology and equipment). They have manually tilled the ground to make it ready for planting their crops. The farmer goes out to spread, or sow, the seeds. To do this they have a pouch on their belt and spread the seed by throwing it into the prepared soils.

Some of the seeds hit the hardened path that the farmer walks on. In these areas, the birds eat up the seeds because they aren't able to make roots.

Some of the seeds fall on rocky places. In these areas, there isn't enough soil for the seed to grow deep roots. These seeds grow quickly but are scorched by the sun and wither.

Some of the seeds land among thorns and weeds. When they sprout up, they live for a while but are eventually choked out.

Some of the seeds reach the good soil. These seeds thrive and produce a crop.

If the soil is the receptiveness of a listener, aka their willingness to learn, what do these four examples show us about how we learn and apply new information? They show us how knowledge evolves into experience.

The seed on the path eaten by birds could be knowledge drowned out by outside influences. A person says they want to learn but they haven't opened themselves to receive or apply new information.

Rocky ground or shallow soil could be a person who initially accepts new information and begins to apply it. But the growth is short-lived. As soon as there is trouble, or the challenge gets difficult they abandon the process.

The seed among thorns I would compare to competing values. There can be practical challenges such as the feeling that one can't invest in a change because their current needs are overwhelming.

It may seem like good soil is a mythical situation. In my experience, good soil means the work has been put in to prepare oneself to receive new information.

Good soil is a result of constant weeding, watering, and caring for the ground. Developing a growth mindset requires you to ensure the soil within you is receptive to the right seeds and influences.

Knowledge combined with **experience** develops into wisdom.

Two Young Pros - 4E's

Let's contrast and compare what two young professionals applying the principles in this book. What would they look like if they were practicing opposite sides of the **Four Elements**?

Young Professional A

Knowledge
Open minded and listening to learn all they can

Experience
Seeking opportunities to be mentored by others

Abilities
Does their best to improve their skills

Resources
Understands that demonstrating their commitment is the key to opening more doors of opportunity

Young Professional B

Close Minded
Unwilling to hear what others are teaching them

Poor Attitude
Dismisses others when they show them how to do something

Lackadaisical
Doesn't give full effort or follow through

Unaccountable
Blames others for their issues rather than taking responsibility

16 Experience

We learn from our experiences. For most of us, we choose to learn the hard way. Learning the hard way is often a long road. The road that takes you from where you are to where you want to be has no shortcuts.

But there are ways you can shorten the time it takes to elevate your **knowledge**, **experience**, and **abilities**.

You can shorten your learning curve by learning from the experiences of others. Rapper KRS One had a sweet and informative interaction with a young YouTuber, *Jazzys WorldTV*. She asked him how hip-hop legends like him could help guide the newer generations. His response builds upon what we are attempting to accomplish in this book.

He says, *"First of all, we've got to guide each other. If older people don't listen to younger people they become slow amongst older people. When younger people don't listen to older people they become slower amongst younger people."*

What a great perspective.

Increasing your knowledge increases your ability to see beyond yourself.

To grow your experiences, you will need input from others.

KRS One explained further, *"If young people listen to older people, they move faster amongst younger people because you have advanced knowledge."*

Knowledge will shorten your DANG learning curve.

You don't have to listen to anyone, but you only harm yourself by refusing to learn from others. If you open yourself to receive knowledge from those who have travelled the path before you, it will help you accelerate your learning journey. Learn from their experiences of *bridging the gaps* in their own lives.

The learning process is not a one-way street. KRS One spoke to those from his generation saying, *"When older people listen to younger people we move faster in the older world because you got new knowledge. So, **when we listen to each other we all grow**."*

He touches on the importance of learning together. For the reader, this means being willing to learn. For the parents, educators, managers, and others supporting young professionals, it means the same.

Whether you are young or old, you will do yourself a great service by keeping an open mind. Being **open minded** means receiving knowledge and learning from the experiences of those around you.

Growing Your Experience

Knowledge: **Increasing**
Experience: **Growing**
Abilities: Low
Resources: Low

How are you observing and applying wisdom to grow your experience?

<u>If you are preparing for an interview</u>
If you have direct experience with roles and responsibilities for the position you are applying for, be prepared to highlight this. If you don't have direct experience, think through your relevant experiences and abilities that would make you a strong contributor to the company. Review Chapters 4-10 for more ideas on how you can prepare for an interview.

<u>If you are trying to advance at work</u>
There are two things to keep in mind when you are trying to get more experience at work.

First, always look to be of value. In construction, we always tell people that if they don't know what to do, grab a broom and sweep. Something always needs to be swept. If your managers see you are always looking to be productive, it will go a long way to forming a positive perception of your work ethic.

The second thing is that to learn you must be open to learning from many different types of people. Sometimes the people that can teach you the most may not have the best communication or presentation skills. This could mean that you must work with somebody you don't particularly like for a short period of time. It is important to make short term sacrifices to gain skills that will help you over the long run.

17 Abilities

I didn't know a lot about what I wanted to do when I graduated high school, but I did know that I wanted to work in construction.

I had <u>some</u> relevant **knowledge**, **experience**, and **abilities**.

For example, I had worked some odd jobs with my uncle who was a contractor. Most of this was helping on various job sites. One standout project was building a large fence with my cousin throughout the summer. If I wanted to work in construction, I knew most of the tools and how to use them safely.

I had a friend who was working in a cabinet shop. Having someone I knew who was **honest** and **hardworking** opened an opportunity to interview with the business owner at their job. Surrounding myself with positive people helped me get a job I enjoyed.

I was able to get an entry-level job in the construction industry. I opened the door to pursue my vision by being in the right place at the right time. I was able to take a risk and within a short time being in a new place, I was employed in the skilled trades.

Increased knowledge

I learned every aspect of the production side of the cabinet business. Starting at the bottom as a helper for closet installations. Being honest at the entry-level means doing what you say, or most often simply showing up every day. Showing up will expose you to opportunities to learn.

Increased experiences

As I successfully helped the installers, I received opportunities to go out on my own as an installer. I built trust with the owner by being a hard worker. The simplest way to build confidence within yourself (internal) and trust with others (external) is through *The Three Be's*.

Increased abilities

I took every opportunity I had to learn a new skill or help in other areas of the business. By doing so I continued to build trust and open doors for myself within the business. Finally, I had built up enough trust that I was given the responsibility to run the production shop. This meant I would prepare all of the kits for our installers.

Remember, the process of increasing your knowledge and experience results in the elevation of your abilities. You must plant the seeds, then water, feed, and weed the soil.

Internally: **Knowledge + Experience = Abilities**

When you put your abilities to the test, you become more productive (internally) which means you are more profitable (externally) for the company. As your trust increases within the organization so does your access to opportunities for increased compensation and career advancement (**resources**).

Developing Your Abilities

Knowledge: **Increasing**
Experience: **Growing**
Abilities: **Developing**
Resources: Low

How are you developing your abilities?

<u>If you are preparing for an interview</u>
If you are starting out, you likely don't have a lot of abilities that directly translate to being of value to a company. Similar to indirect experience discussed in the prior chapter, highlight the skills and abilities that you have that will help you be successful in the company you are applying for. Review Chapters 4-10 for more ideas on how you can prepare for an interview.

<u>If you are trying to advance at work</u>
Your skill and efficiency should be developing daily. The activities you perform day in and day out are the ones that you should become more precise, quicker, and more adept at performing.

For example, if you assemble parts for a widget, if you started out completing 4 units a day, it should take a few work cycles for you to add one more. Often what makes you more effective at work is being more efficient.

Being more efficient involves eliminating waste. This means you understand how to set yourself, your tools, and your workspace up to perform your work with the least amount of wasted actions or energy.

18 Resources

For the most part, **abilities** are what you develop internally. **Resources** are what you develop externally. Resources includes everything from the people and influences in your life to your access to money, education, opportunities, and tools. Understanding what you need to get from one stage of life to the other is like cooking a good meal.

What is your favorite food?

What makes this meal appealing to you?

What emotions do the odors of this food usher into your recollection?

While it likely has a lot to do with the taste it likely also involves many of your other senses. In addition to flavor, your favorite food excites memories of the atmosphere and people around you when you first sampled it.

If preparing to *thrive* were comparable to creating a meal, your vision would be to produce the taste, odor, and atmosphere that drew you to the dish. Your goal would be to assemble the ingredients necessary to facilitate the dining experience. As with most things in life, there is more than one way to go about this process. Let's start with two obvious options.

Option 1: Start with a plan (goals)

If you see a cool recipe online you may start with a fixed goal for what you would like to eat. You may not have all of the ingredients, but the recipe provides a plan to work from. When you make a meal, it may not look as pretty as what a social media influencer created, but it can still be excellent.

The same goes for building from the blueprint you have observed in others, you won't look exactly like someone else. But you're cooking your dish and your knowledge will grow the more you expose yourself to new experiences.

Option 2: Start with an idea (vision)

If you've tasted something before and want to recreate it, you may look up a recipe (Option 1) or try to build it from scratch using your senses as your guide. If Option 1 is knowledge-based, Option 2 is experience-based.

The act of cooking can be as joyous as the experience of eating what is produced, even if the cooking experiment fails to achieve its intended outcome.

I find that in the personal and professional experiments throughout my life, I usually have some general ideas about what I want to achieve.

I don't always know what I want my *dish* to look like, but my past experiments have provided me with a framework that shortens my learning curve each time I try something new. It starts by surrounding myself with resources, people, and experiences that help me learn more about what I'm trying to *cook* next.

Option 3: Start with what you have (resources)

For many of us who grew up with fewer resources, we became adept at making the most with a little. Growing up my family was on food stamps. This meant the government gave us funny-looking paper money that looked like it came from the game of Monopoly. It made it obvious that your family was on assistance and that was embarrassing at times for me as a child.

When the market crashed in 2008/2009, what many people refer to as *The Great Recession*, I was an adult with four children to feed. Our finances dried up and I had to humble myself to request food assistance. This time around our benefits were provided through a debit card which was much less obvious than the paper money from my childhood.

Growing up and as an adult, my family needed help. There is nothing wrong with asking for help and receiving assistance. The goal for me growing up was to not be in a place of need, not because I looked down on my past but because I wanted to build something more for myself. As an adult, I was crushed because about a year and a half prior I had started my own business. I took a big risk in stepping out as an entrepreneur and I felt like I failed.

Thankfully people around us helped us a lot. I was able to get odd jobs here and there to try to keep things together financially. In this instance, all I could do was work hard wherever I had the opportunity. It was difficult and took a long time to get back to where we weren't extremely tight with our money. Life can kick you in the gut, so it's important to keep fighting.

Back to my point about starting with what you have. Have you heard, "Necessity is the mother of invention"? It means that often creativity and innovation are born from tough times. One night we were pretty light on food and options, but we wanted to make the most of our evening together as a family. I took some of the supplies we had including tortillas, beans, cheese, and rice. I assembled them differently, creating what we called *tortilla pizzas*. They loved it.

To this day our kids still enjoy this meal. Thankfully they were young enough that they only remember what my wife and I did to make the food, the atmosphere, and the night enjoyable rather than understanding how serious our circumstances were.

Now, when we make this dish, the kids remember when we first introduced it while my wife and I reflect on how we made the most of our limited resources. Food has an interesting way of bringing all of our senses to the table.

Positive examples from others have a way of encouraging us to think differently about what is possible. It's important to remember that many times in your life preparing to **thrive** will require making the most of what you have, regardless of how little that seems.

Shortening Your DANG
Learning Curve

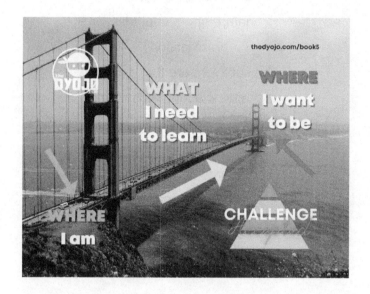

To *Bridge the Gap* between where
you are and where you want to be,
focus on what you need to learn.

You cannot shortcut the path
to increasing your
knowledge, **experiences**,
abilities, and **resources**.

But, you can shorten the time it takes
to bridge many of the gaps
in your professional skills.

To survive and even thrive

in a changing world,

nature offers another

great lesson:

the survivors are those who

at the least adapt to change,

or even better learn to

benefit from change

and grow intellectually

and personally.

That means careful listening

and constant learning.

Frances Arnold

19 Time

What is the most valuable resource in life? Value is related to how precious something is. The most valuable things are in short supply or cannot be replaced. What resources can you "spend" but are unable to acquire more? You may be tempted to think it's money but if you spend money, you can make more.

There's <u>at least</u> one thing more valuable than money.

Time is one of those un-replenishable resources. Once you use a unit of time there is no way to get it back. So, time is one of the most important resources that you have at your disposal. Time should be treated with great respect because it is in limited supply.

Put a picture in your mind of the cliff you are standing on (where you are). There's a wide distance, with water or a great void, separating you from the cliff you want to reach (where you want to be). Moving across this massive distance requires a bridge.

This is why we refer to the journey from where you are to where you want to be as *bridging the gap*.

There is no shortcut across this bridge.

You cannot shortcut the path to increasing your **knowledge**, **experiences**, **abilities**, and **resources**. But you can shorten the time it takes to bridge many of the gaps in your professional skills. Many people use 10,000 hours as the amount of time it takes to get good at something. Whether it's this number or not, you cannot shorten the total hours, but you can reduce the length of time it takes.

For example, if you were trying to learn to play the guitar, and it takes 10,000 hours to "master" this new skill, you can approach this goal in a variety of ways.

> Committing one hour a day, or 7 hours a week, will take you 10,000 days, or 952 weeks, or 27 years.

When learning a skill, shortening that timeframe would be any extra hours in a week that you can commit to your goal.

> If you can add half an hour a day, you are now committing 10.5 hours a week, and reducing the total length of time to 952 weeks or 18.5 years. An extra half an hour a day or 3.5 hours a week can shave off 8.5 years.

To learn something new you can shorten your DANG learning curve in two ways. First, by elevating your level of commitment (output), even by a slight increase. Second, by the quality of your inputs.

> Input: Those influences from outside of yourself that increase your knowledge, experience, and abilities.

> Output: Those elements from within yourself such as being honest, hardworking, and willing to learn.

Surround yourself with people who want to see you succeed. These same people should be able to speak honestly when you are headed down the wrong path or getting in your own way.

Expanding Your Resources

Knowledge: **Increasing**
Experience: **Growing**
Abilities: **Developing**
Resources: **Expanding**

How are you making the most of your time to expand your resources?

<u>If you are preparing for an interview</u>
The tools you have available to you are primarily accessed through the Internet. You can research the company. Find articles about the organization. Review social media. All of these resources help you to be prepared for your interview. Review Chapters 4-10 for more ideas on how you can prepare for an interview.

<u>If you are trying to advance at work</u>
Most companies have a training and development process. Some companies have done a better job of making their process clear. An organization that has a detailed process should empower you to work through the steps for advancement.

If you are part of an organization that doesn't have as detailed of a process, you will want to speak with your supervisor to ask what you can do to advance. It's always a good idea to ask about the development process in your interview and continue to explore it as you gain experience in the company.

20 Making Mistakes

You will fail and you will make plenty of mistakes. When you fail in a work scenario, most bosses won't expect you to be perfect, but they will value taking accountability. When faced with the reality of making a mistake there are two choices:

Young Professional A

> Tries to cover up or ignore their mistake.
>
> Looks for someone else to blame.
>
> Doesn't learn from the situation and likely will repeat it.

Young Professional B

> Makes their supervisor aware of the issue.
>
> Takes personal responsibility.
>
> Identifies what they did wrong and what they will do in the future to prevent a repeat.

<u>An honest mistake can be corrected, but someone unwilling to admit or face their failures is hard to fix</u>. Most supervisors, managers, and business owners will be upset with Young Professional A. They could face discipline, suspension, or being fired. You may feel that hiding from the issue or blaming someone else will work in your favor but ultimately it won't. It's better to be honest.

Those same people will respect Young Professional B's willingness to take ownership. When you make a mistake, admit that you are in the wrong. You will do even better if you communicate what you need to do to prevent the same mistake from happening again. Employers don't want to fire you, but they need you to do your job to the best of your ability. **Being willing to learn includes learning from your mistakes.**

Most supervisors don't like surprises. If you make a mistake and try to hide it, the consequences will only be worse. If you tell your supervisor about the issue, they can formulate a plan and work with you to address the issue.

I can remember getting a call from a customer who came home to discover they had a missing lamp. At first, they thought it may have been moved as a subcontractor was doing some painting work that day. They soon discovered that the lamp was broken and hidden behind the couch. That doesn't sound good, does it? It looks like a cover-up.

Because whoever broke the lamp didn't inform us, we were unable to get ahead of the issue. I could have made a simple call, *"I apologies but I need to inform you, our team damaged a lamp while they were painting. Do you have any information on where we could find a replacement for you?"* Being *proactive* is so much better than being *reactive*.

It turned out that the lamp was just a basic model that was available locally. We were able to make things right by replacing the lamp and apologizing. It would have been so much better for someone to take responsibility. Having the information, even bad news, would have helped us be proactive in restoring the damage.

It's unrealistic for anyone to expect that you won't make mistakes or even fail. People often think of being honest, or having integrity, in terms of not telling lies. Honesty is also expressed in accountability, which means you own up to it when you make a mistake.

"I have not failed 10,000 times,
I've successfully found
10,000 ways that will not work."

Thomas Edison

Swimming in the
Deep End

Learning new things feels like
swimming in the deep end.

The deeper you go,
the more you discover new things.

21 Living in Your Means

When you start out in the workforce you will struggle to cover your financial needs. You will need to be disciplined with how you spend your money if you want to move beyond living paycheck-to-paycheck. I tell my kids all the time that if they can control their spending habits and keep themselves out of debt, they can significantly reduce the pressure to work.

We call this living <u>within</u> your means. For example, if you have low living costs for shelter, food, and clothing by making choices to survive on the essentials, you may be able to get by on a 40-hour work week (maybe less). 40 hours a week at one job, or five 8-hour long workdays, is considered a full time job.

Living *within* your means:

> Only spending what you make.

> Keeping your costs low so that you don't have to work as long/hard.

> Ideally spending less than what you make so that you can save towards long-term goals.

If you were born into a family with strong finances, you may not have to work. Or the pressure to work that may be significantly different than most of your peers. For most of us, we work because we need to. Many people must work harder (or longer) than necessary because they have made life choices that have increased their responsibilities. We call this living <u>outside</u> of your means.

Living *outside* your means:

> Spending more than you make.

> Allowing your costs to exceed your current level of earning meaning you take on debt or have to work more hours to try to make up the gap.

> Rather than saving money you are taking on debt which makes the hole deeper.

Making money is not the same thing as ***thriving***. Money is an important resource. If you learn to use it wisely it can help you reach your goal.

Setting & Achieving Goals

You can build your goals from (X) start to the desired finish or (Z) from the destination back to the starting point. Young Worker A and Young Worker B both have a goal to save $1,000.00. Let's say they both want to put a deposit down on a car.

Young Professional A
Decides to map out their goal by choosing Path (X) from their current starting point on through to their anticipated finish

Start = $0.00 in savings

By next paycheck
Young Worker A can put $25.00 into savings

If they continue to do this every two weeks,
Young Worker A will have on average $50.00 a month in savings

It will take them 20 paychecks or 10 months to reach the goal of saving $1,000.00

Young Professional B
Has a goal to save $1,000.00 in six months. They decide to map out their goal by choosing Path (Z) from the destination back to the starting point

End = $1,000.00 in six months

$1,000.00 divided by six (months) = $166.67 per month

Creating a roadmap or written plan is a good way to keep yourself accountable to achieving your goals. Making smart money decisions is an essential habit if you want to *thrive*.

22 Enjoy the Process

Becoming the person you want to be, also referred to as achieving your potential, is a lifelong pursuit. Daily following through with your mindsets and habits. You have to feed, seed, and pull the weeds if you are going to blossom into the person you want to be.

Thriving is not just a destination, it's a process.

For example, if you want to learn how to become a carpenter you wouldn't enroll in a gardening course. The gardening class could teach you many good things but it would not help you become a skilled woodworker.

Being willing to learn is important because it is possible to be **hardworking** but doing things wrong.

As you acquire **knowledge**, putting this information to use increases your level of **experience**. Yet, this time and effort can be wasted. In an extreme example, if you were attempting to drive a nail with a screwdriver, you may eventually get the thing done but it would be an exhausting use of time.

> The right tool, used the right way, would help you achieve the goal much quicker.
>
> Developing the right mindset helps develop the right habits for success.
>
> Your actions affect your outcomes.

The wrong mindset can lead to the wrong habits. In the nail driving example, this person might have been eager to learn but was either unwilling to listen to direction or started with their limited perspective.

Being willing to learn means being willing to listen, to research, to observe, and to be taught. *Bridging the Gap* isn't just one fixed destination, there are many bridges along the journey. Each bridge you cross, each learning curve you shorten, reveals another bridge. We are all a continuous work in progress.

> ***Success is not a <u>destination</u> that you reach***
> ***and the journey is over.***
> ***Success is not an <u>object</u> that you obtain***
> ***and the challenge is complete.***

If success were a fixed <u>destination</u>, we'd cross one bridge, and the journey would be over. Where's the fun in that? For example, some people think you go to college to be successful. We know that's not true. It's not as simple as going to college and *snapping* your fingers into becoming an instant success.

If success were an <u>object</u>, we'd find it and the challenge would be complete. What would we do then? For example, every sports fan wants their team to win a championship. If a team wins one time, does it mean the team gets swept into the clouds forever to be celebrated as the ultimate winner? No. They enjoy the moment and eventually, they have to start the next season trying to do it again.

It's important to be driven but it's as important to have the right balance in your life. There are a lot of people who have reached the pinnacle of their careers, accumulated wealth, and have everything a person could dream of, <u>yet</u> they are miserable.

One thing that can lead to misery is having a fixed perspective on success. It's important to have goals, but it's also important to adapt as you acquire new knowledge and experience.

It's important to enjoy the process.

Self Discipline

In the segment on *Creating and Achieving Goals*, we discussed two ways to map out your plan. For both scenarios, if the young professionals want to achieve their goals in six months or less they will need to find ways to:

Increase their inputs (credits) and make more money

Decrease their outputs (debits) and spend less money

Or, a combination of both

Decrease. If either will make some sacrifices over the next six months, they can reach their goal within their time frame. If either used to spend $7.00 at least three times a week on buying coffee, that's a $21.00 a week habit. If either of them can move that $21.00 a week from the debit column to the savings column. This simple change of habit can bring them closer to their goals.

Increase. If either can pick up 4 extra hours a week at $15.00 per hour, that's $60.00 a week that they can add to the credit column.

Combined. By making small sacrifices to decrease their spending habits as well as doing what they can to pick up extra work they are moving closer to their goal. In just one week, these two small changes combined would move them close to the halfway point for the month by adding $81.00 (before taxes) to the desired outcome.

Developing self-discipline allows you to focus on your vision and achieve your goals.

23 A Unique Perspective

We often take modern conveniences for granted. Everything we use was invented and improved by someone. Every invention starts with the same thought, "What if..." But you know these inventors and innovators didn't achieve success overnight. Invention and innovation require a commitment of time.

I enjoy learning from history. As we wrap up this first book in the Challenge Accepted series, I'll share an example of an someone who spent a lot of time failing to make something we use every day.

This figure from history had the persistence to work through setbacks and frustrations to create something we use every day.

If you have this book in your hands, you are able to see it because there is some form of lighting. If you're like me, you take indoor lighting for granted. It's not something you think about. You just turn the switch on, and the room is illuminated.

Do you know the story of the invention of the modern lightbulb?

Several decades ago, indoor lighting was provided by candlelight or oil lamps. A man named Thomas Edison had the bright idea that he could illuminate the world. The only problem with his idea was that he could not find a filament, one of the key internal components, that would allow his lightbulb to last more than a few hours.

The Franklin Institute states,

"*In the period from 1878 to 1880 Edison and his associates worked on at least three thousand different theories to develop an efficient incandescent lamp. Incandescent lamps make light by using electricity to heat a thin strip of material (called a filament) until it gets hot enough to glow[iv].*"

Edison was conducting his experiments from 1878 to 1880, how long ago was that?

If you are reading this in 2024, you would subtract 1880, and the magic number is **144** years ago.

When was the last time you had to change a lightbulb? For most of us they are just there. They are expected to work. This modern convenience didn't happen by chance. Someone had to believe it was possible and try day after day to make it a reality.

Nearly one hundred and fifty years ago, Edison and his team spent <u>over two years</u> experimenting with <u>thousands</u> of tiny filaments.

In the process of experimentation and discovery, knowing what doesn't work is as important as what eventually does work. If you want to know what works or how to solve a problem, you can start by testing the things you think will work (hypothesis).

Each failed attempt eliminates the things that don't work. One by one we scratch the things that don't work from the list. Each time we fail, we can combat our desire to quit by understanding that we are one step closer to discovering what will work.

This is called **the process of elimination.**

After trying and trying and trying various experiments, thereby failing and failing and failing, Edison would say, "*I have not failed 10,000 times—I've successfully found 10,000 ways that will not work.*"

After a year he had his first successful bulb, but it would only burn for a few hours. By 1880 he finally had a bulb that would burn for nearly fifteen hours. Imagine committing two years of your life to daily experiments. Laboring over various small fibers needed to make something work from a few minutes to finally illuminating just over half a day.

Edison sacrificed his time and effort in the short term (nearsighted) and ended up making a huge long-term impact on the world (farsighted).

I would imagine he thought about quitting after 100 trials, but he didn't. What would your breaking point have been? The last time you started something, how long did you give the effort before you called it quits? Was it a few days? Was it a month?

When you face an obstacle or adversity, it's not time to quit, it's time to deepen your commitment to figuring out the answer. Each time he failed; Edison's mindset was that he was getting one step closer to the answer he was searching for.

Being **hardworking** to grow your abilities and **willing to learn** to grow your **knowledge** is a commitment you must renew every day.

Thomas kept the right mindset and habits even when it seemed, over and over, that things were not working. I believe ol' Tom would agree that *you don't need to be exceptional to make a difference in this world.*

Thomas

This picture shows inventor Thomas Edison and one of his light bulbs. The Franklin Institute states, "In the period from 1878 to 1880 Edison and his associates worked on at least three thousand different theories to develop an efficient incandescent lamp." I would imagine he thought about quitting after 100 trials, but he didn't. What would your breaking point have been?

24 Effort

As we discussed in Chapter 12, you don't need superpowers to *thrive* in the modern workplace. What you will need is a growth mindset and consistent effort (habits).

For most of us, how we do one thing is also how we approach most things.

If you are like Young Professional B from the examples in this book (see *Two Young Pro's*), your limited mindset and low-quality habits will bleed into your work.

If you are like Young Professional A from the same section, your open mindset and willingness to learn will help you achieve in the workplace.

Even if you don't have a majestic green mullet or five fancy rings, you can make a difference in this world. Positive impact does <u>not</u> require superhuman abilities or effort. Positive impact requires intentionally developing your abilities and putting in (*at minimum*) above-average effort.

That said, please <u>don't</u> measure your success by whether you are better than your peers. It's easy to pick someone who is flailing and tell yourself, *"At least I'm not like so-and-so."* Being better than people who have no vision, goals, or discipline isn't much to brag about.

Making yourself feel good by comparing yourself to people with low effort won't get you very far.

Effort compounds. Meaning the more you practice honesty, hard work, and a willingness to learn, the stronger you become in those things.

If you are willing to study just <u>a bit</u> more than your classmates, put in <u>a few</u> extra reps than your teammates, or do the things no one else is willing to do at work, you will set yourself up for opportunities that few others will have. In Chapter 14 I shared an example of how this worked in my career.

To be clear, if you want to be exceptional, putting in the bare minimum will <u>not</u> get you there. Being the best, or the greatest of all time (G.O.A.T.), requires a level of commitment that few are willing to put in. Even those who have been the best at their craft, whether in sports, business, science, art, etc., would tell you they had to work their butts off and learn from others.

Whenever you try something new to improve yourself, give it 90 days. You need this much time, daily trying a little harder at whatever you are doing, to see whether it produces the result you are striving for.

Increasing your effort is essential to thriving in the modern workplace.

> **Listen** <u>a little</u> better so you can hear what is going on around you and identify what may have been there the whole time just waiting for you to notice.

> **Look** <u>a little</u> closer at things that have been happening around you so you can see more clearly.

> **Try** even just <u>a little</u> bit harder and see if that level of effort doesn't spill over into multiple areas of your life.

The journey from doing it right to doing it excellently is often a series of small but meaningful habits.

Let's use math to demonstrate the value of increasing your level of effort (even marginally). This will show the benefits of trying something new compared to maintaining a mediocre level of effort.

If you have the same mindset and habits with <u>no increase</u> in effort over the next 365 days (a year) you will make a net change of zero. Mathematically this looks like 1.00 (zero increase in effort) to the power of 365 (1.00^{365}) = 1.00 (zero increase in output)

If you just add a <u>small increase</u> in effort to elevate your mindset and improve your habits over the next 365 days (a year) you will make a significantly greater positive change. Mathematically this looks like 1.01 (.01 increase in effort) to the power of 365 (1.01^{365}) = 37.7 (increase in output).

Mathematically, adding a tenth of a percent (input) to your daily effort would yield a 37.7-point increase in positive change (output).

This one percent increase in effort won't get you to excellence but it will bring you closer. If you want to be a person who *seizes the day* (see Chapter 14) you have to first plant the seeds.

It is important to develop the right habits as early and consistently as possible.

If you want to **earn** more, you need to **learn** more.

The quicker you get started, the sooner you'll achieve your next goal.

As you continue to elevate your effort, day after day, results will follow.

Effort Leads to Results

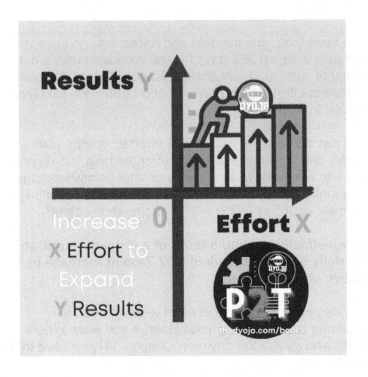

Listen <u>a little</u> better

Look <u>a little</u> closer

Try <u>a little</u> bit harder

You surround yourself
with amazing,
grade-A talent,
and you're going
to have to lift your game.
You kind of thrive
just by being around
such people.

Joe Lo Truglio

25 Leaving The Right Way

We can't talk about preparing for and building a career without addressing the right way to leave a job. It's important to understand that it takes a lot of resources to hire and onboard a new employee. Employers want to see that you start a job and stay with it long enough to be of value to their organization.

If you've had several jobs with short durations, you are going to be asked about it. Why is that? For many employers it looks like you bounce around. People who quickly jump from job to job can appear to be unreliable.

Leaving is not wrong, but it's important to understand business owner's perceptions. Before you leave a job, make sure the decisions you make in the short term (nearsighted) also make sense for your long-term goals (farsighted).

Before you make big decisions, ask yourself, *"How easily can I explain my reasons for making this change?"*

Some work environments are not the right fit. If the environment is unsafe and you have given your best effort to make a positive impact, it may be time to leave. I can tell you that I have been in some bad working environments and several more that were dysfunctional. I find that my mindset has great power in determining whether my outlook and effort are positively applied.

Having a growth mindset means giving one hundred percent (be hardworking) and learning what you can from everyone.

How you leave a job is important. It can say a lot about the type of person you are. If you decide to leave, unless the conditions are unsafe, do your best to leave the right way. This often means giving a two-week notice to your employer. It's generally good practice but isn't required by law.

Many employers expect this type of notice even they don't follow it when they let people go. It is wise to confirm with your new employer that if the former employer lets you go before the two weeks, they are ready to bring you on right away.

Leaving on good terms means that you are respectful in how you announce your plans for departure and that you don't burn bridges. You never know when you may have to walk across that same bridge. Or you may come across people from your past who play a role in achieving your future goals.

For example, what if the person you told off at a job you hated is now a key member of the hiring panel for a job you really want? Would you regret how you left if you had to face them again?

In the same way that you want your supervisors to treat you as an individual and not assume the worst about you, it's important to give your bosses the same grace.

You may think a supervisor doesn't get you or doesn't get *anything*, but later find out they weren't as bad as you thought.

Before you jump ship, make sure that you aren't handicapping yourself by not learning all that you can.

Do what is right for you while being mindful of the potential consequences of your decisions. Keep your long-term vision (nearsighted) in mind as you achieve your short-term goals (farsighted).

Additional Resources

This is a short list of additional resources we are familiar with, including organizations, podcasts, books, etc.

Organizations

Bring Back The Trades - **bringbackthetrades.org** - Helping to fund scholarships for trade school students.

Explore the Trades - **explorethetrades.org** - Committed to developing the next generation of a skilled workforce by changing the perception of the trades.

Kickass Careers - **kickasscareers.ca** - Teach the young hands of today to build the world of tomorrow.

The DYOJO - **thedyojo.com** - Helping contractors shorten their DANG learning curve through podcasts, books, and content.

Super Tech University - **morningtechmeeting.com** - Teaching technicians the "soft skills" they need to be successful in the field.

Working Class - **working--class.org** - Making the trades cool again.

Podcasts

Blue Collar Nation - Dedicated to making the lives of blue collar service businesses better.

Blue Is The New White - Host Josh Zolin wants everyone to know there is more than one path to a stable career and a great financial future.

Learning and Missteps - Jesse and Rene dig into the stories of the men and women who have built careers in the construction industry.

Restoration Today - Host Michelle Blevins covers everything restoration-related.

Sweat and Grime - Bryan, Rick, Matt, and Greg sit and discuss a variety of topics loosely based on the skilled trades.

The DYOJO Podcast - Helping contractors shorten their DANG learning curve.

Books

Adjuster's Resume Playbook: A Step by Step Guide to Creating an Insurance Adjuster Resume by Chris Stanley. This book is a step-by-step guide of how to craft your resume as a qualified candidate for an insurance adjuster job regardless of how much experience you have handling claims.

Blue is the New White: The Best Path to Success No One Told You About - Until Now by Josh Zolin. There is more than one path to a stable career and a great financial future; in this book, you'll learn just how many opportunities await you in places you never thought to look.

Dream Big! How to Reach for Your Stars by Abigail Harrison. From Astronaut Abby, the dynamic founder of The Mars Generation, comes a book about dreaming big, reaching for the stars, and planning for success!

Get Out of the Truck: Build the Business You Always Dreamed About by Idan Shpizear. What you will find are insights on the most important elements for building a successful business.

Girls Who Build by Marisa L. Richards. From Lucy the Laborer to Winnie the Welder, learn what it takes to build our homes and cities from this inspiring group of girls.

A Larger Loss: A Thriller by Ryan Reese. This fiction book has birthed the restoration thriller sub-genre, captivating readers with every storytelling twist and turn.

Insuring Tomorrow: Engaging Millennials in the Insurance Industry by Tony Canas and Carly Burnham. This is your guidebook to not only keep your Millennials but grow them and help them fall in love with the insurance industry.

So, You Want To Be A Project Manager: Mindsets and Habits for Growth by Jon Isaacson. This book is a primer on the mindset and habits for success as a project manager.

The House She Built by Mollie Elkman & Georgia Castellano. This book educates young readers about all the people and skills that go into building a home.

The Misleading Money Mantra: How Chasing Money Is Holding You Back From the Life and Business of Your Dreams by Chris Stanley. This book will change the way you see investing and will make you feel good about investing in your life, not just your bank account.

Unqualified Success: Bridging the Gap From Where You Are Today to Where You Want to Be to Achieve Massive Success by Rachel Stewart. No matter who you are or what your circumstances are, *Unqualified Success* will give you practical and real tools that can be implemented today to achieve your goals.

Working Class: Making the Trades Cool Again by Nick Kasick. The TV show Working Class was developed to bring attention to the epidemic shortage of skilled trades professionals, and to promote vocational careers.

About the Author

My daughter took this picture in 2023, many of our friends say we look like a rock band.

Jon Isaacson, *The Intentional Restorer*, is a contractor, author, and host of **The DYOJO Podcast**. His organization, The DYOJO, helps contractors shorten their DANG learning curve. He has been in the skilled trades for over 20 years. Jon has helped start, grow, and revive various service-based teams throughout property restoration and the skilled trades. He is currently the Vice President of Operations for **ARES** in Puyallup, Washington.

More from The DYOJO

Book 1
Be Intentional: Estimating
"This book was both fun and educational to read. It should be in every restorer's library next to the standards. **- Randy Carley**

Book 2
Be Intentional: Culture
"This book provides so many different insights that the reader can understand where everyone in a team is coming from, not just from people in a position of management. The information and experience from all walks of life paints a clear picture on how people can approach leadership." - **David Smith**

Book 3
So, You Want To Be A Project Manager?
"This book covers all the good, the bad, and the ugly of being a Project Manager. The information was so well laid out and processed that I keep extra copies in my office now to hand out to those that I know will benefit from it." - **Gordy Powell**

Book 4
How To Suck Less At Estimating
"Jon truly has amazing insight into all facets of property restoration. His delivery is straightforward and provides very valuable information. Do yourself a favor and get all of his books. You will not regret it!" - **Keith Nelson**

The DYOJO Podcast
Thursdays are for **The DYOJO Podcast** - *Helping Contractors Shorten Their DANG Learning Curve.* YouTube and Spotify.

PropertyRestorationHistory.com

This is a labor of love. We are working to track down and piece together elements of the history and rise of the property restoration industry. This effort will include aspects of carpet cleaners becoming water damage mitigation specialists, the evolution of fire damage restoration, the integration of insurance claims repairs, and the emergence of what we now call property restoration professionals.

Additional Thanks Yous

Thank you to co-editor Tiffany Acuff for her patience in working alongside The DYOJO. Finding herself in the restoration industry by chance with zero knowledge, she found some inspiration from my first book and has been helping me edit every book since. She has a passion for learning and elevating the property restoration industry which fuels her efforts to help me edit my ramblings.

Thank you to those who took time out of their busy schedules to peer-review portions of this book and provide incredibly helpful and honest feedback (including the testimonials at the opening) which contributed to improving the content you have just consumed.

Endnotes and References

i Aresrestoration.com
ii Proverbs 24:32
iii This story is adapted from the Parable of the Sower in Matthew 13:1-23
iv Read more about Thomas Edison and the light bulb - https://www.fi.edu/en/science-and-education/collection/edisons-lightbulb

The DYOJO Podcast

Helping Contractors Shorten

Their DANG Learning Curve

thedyojo.com/podcast

YouTube, Apple, & Spotify

Made in the USA
Monee, IL
20 January 2024

51335363R00075